Books by Fran Stewart

Fiction

The Biscuit McKee Mystery Series

Orange as Marmalade
Yellow as Legal Pads
Green as a Garden Hose
Blue as Blue Jeans
Indigo as an Iris
Violet as an Amethyst
Gray as Ashes
Red as a Rooster
Black as Soot
Pink as a Peony
White as Ice

A Slaying Song Tonight

Turnaround

The ScotShop Mysteries

A Wee Murder in My Shop
A Wee Dose of Death
A Weee Homicide in the Hotel

Poetry
Resolution

For Children

As Orange As Marmalade/
Tan naranja como Mermelada
(a bilingual book)

Non-Fiction

From The Tip of My Pen: a workbook
for writers

BeesKnees
A six volume series..

BeesKnees BeeKeeping #1: A Beekeep-
ing Memoir
BeesKnees Beekeeping #2: ...
BeesKnees Beekeeping #3: ...
BeesKnees Beekeeping #4: ...
BeesKnees Beekeeping #5: ...
BeesKnees Beekeeping #6: ...

The Clear Series

Clear as Mud
Clearly Me
Crystal Clear

After I Die: What My Executor Will
Need to Know   http://bit.ly/AfterIDie

Your Life Your Stories: How to write
your memoirs

YouTube

Oh Wow—Green Funerals
https://bit.ly/GreenFunerals

My Own Ship Press

YOUR LIFE
YOUR STORIES:

How to write
your
memoirs

FRAN STEWART

Your Life Your Stories: How to write your memoirs

franstewart.com

ISBN: 978-1-951368-54-8

This book was printed in the United States of America.

Published by
My Own Ship Press
Lawrenceville GA

For Marcia, for always being there

And for my grandchildren, so they'll get where I'm coming from

Author's Note

So often, I find that the people who take my memoirs-writing classes do it because they've suddenly realized that their time on this earth is beginning to be somewhat more limited than they once thought.

Duh!

But let's look at this a different way. The British novelist and poet Mary Webb (1881-1927) once wrote:

> The reality of death is neither to be questioned nor feared.
> Death is a dark dream, but it is not a nightmare.

Let's approach the whole topic of writing our stories with this in mind. These stories reflect our adventures with this life we're fortunate enough to have. And let's thank the creatures (both human and non-human) who've made our lives more worthwhile than they would have been if we'd been going it alone.

I have so many reasons for gratitude.

My family, who have put up with my vagaries for more years than I can believe, and who love me anyway.

My dear friends, particularly Marcia, Darlene, Melanie, Drew, Debbie, and Karen, who have endured the carping I'm (unfortunately) prone to at times, and who love me anyway.

Lyn Asselta, the amazing artist whose weekly newsletter has uplifted me and brought me comfort and hope every Saturday morning. I highly suggest signing up for it at http://lynasselta.com You will not regret it, I promise. I also have to thank her for graciously allowing me to quote from two of her newsletters (see chapters 12 and 14).

And finally, Mona Leiter, who provided all the technical expertise for my YouTube presentation about green funerals: https://bit.ly/GreenFunerals

Table of Contents

Types of Flight   Joy
Who/What/Where I left   The Pool: Aftermath to Divorce
Behind   Somebody Said a Mother...
Why I'm a Dandelion   Yellow Angel Stories
My Too-Late Note

Fran Stewart

Chapter 1 Why Bother?

Have you always wanted to write the stories of your life, but never had any idea how to get started? Are your children, grandchildren, nieces, or nephews bugging you to write your stories? Do you feel nobody cares about your stories?

Believe me. Every person has stories worth telling. No matter who you are or what you've been through, your stories deserve to be shared.

When people write their stories, they learn to value their lives and to appreciate the lessons they've learned through all the stories they've lived. When *you* write *your* stories, you delve deeper into the reasons you're alive, the differences you've made in the lives of others, and the ways you've been impacted by the conscious or unconscious actions of others.

If you're ready to capture your most important life lessons – for yourself, your family, and your community – then this is the book for you. It's full of fun and practical writing strategies you can implement immediately.

No writing experience? No problem. All you need is a pen, paper (or computer), and a willingness to try.

You'll end up with a clear path and the confidence to continue to transform your memories into engaging tales that future generations will cherish.

Fran Stewart

Chapter 2 What This Book Isn't

There's a whole slew of published books out there, written by Hollywood stars, tech giants, people who've made headline news, or even by non-famous people who've survived natural disasters, people who've climbed unscalable mountains, folks who have dealt with invasive diseases. Each **memoir** (note the singular) is a book with a specific theme, such as saving a herd of elephants (*Elephant Whisperer* by Lawrence Anthony), living for a year on locally grown foods (*Animal, Vegetable, Miracle* by Barbara Kingsolver), interviewing and learning from an old-time radio sportscaster (*Fridays with Red* by Bob Edwards), or learning to live with and overcome depression (*Depression Visible: the Ragged Edge* by Diana Alishouse).

If you'd like to write a story like that, this is not the book for you, although you *can* get a lot of great suggestions here about how to make your narrative more lively, more interesting, more vivid.

I'm not here to teach you how to write the next best-selling memoir. We'll deal with more than just one theme in your life. We'll be talking about the multiple events of your life:

o   the day your dog ate your birthday cake
o   the day you met your future spouse
o   the first time you had a friend die
o   the way you felt when you held your first child
o   the day you were chased by an emu at a petting zoo
o   or your reaction when you received an unwelcome health diagnosis

If you've taken one of my memoirs classes, either in-person or online, you will have shared many of your stories with the other class members. You may have bought this book to give to a friend or relative. Rest assured that I will NEVER repeat the stories you've told me.

That said, you may feel that some of the stories I cite here in this book, do reflect *your* stories. No, they don't. And yes, they may.

I happen to disagree with Leo Tolstoy's assertion that "*all happy families are alike; each unhappy family is unhappy in its own way.*"

If you grew up in an unhappy family, you'll know that there are numerous ways in which children can be ignored, unappreciated, discounted, abused. If those things happened to you, you'll naturally feel that your childhood was unique. But guess what? Your exact details may be different than anyone else's, but unhappy is unhappy, abuse is

Fran Stewart

abuse, and lack of appreciation affects every child who experiences it.

The very same thing is true if you had a happy family. You'll have had similar experiences to others who grew up loved and appreciated. You'll also have your unique experiences, the ones that are told around the Thanksgiving table. But, again, guess what? Lots of other happy families have the same sorts of stories. The precise details differ (and therein lies the value of telling *your* story), but the overriding themes may very well be the same.

So don't worry about the examples I give. I've made up every one of them (or used examples from my own memoirs). When I've borrowed some ideas from past class members, I've changed all sorts of details. You may recognize your feelings or your motivations in many of these stories, because every family is alike, AND each family is unique.

One final note before we start. If you've bought this book in its physical form, you're welcome to make notes in the margins. If you have the digital version, you can annotate the pages. Or, just keep all your comments, reminders, and notes in a separate folder. Loose papers, three-ring binder, whatever. The form doesn't matter. The writing *does*!

Chapter 3 – Where Do I Start?

Think about your favorite stories from childhood. Didn't a lot of them start with *Once upon a time...*? That's just how you can think of the stories you're about to begin writing. These will be the once-upon-a-time moments of your life. So, let's begin by investigating the way memories are evoked by the five senses: smell, touch, taste, sound, and sight. Doing this will add richness to your stories.

Be sure you write without worrying about what people will think about it. There's always time later to add, subtract, or simply change your sentences.

Now, let's consider just one of the senses: TASTE. Jot down a few words that come to mind when you think of a taste that had some particular meaning to you. Try to think of at least three tastes from your past. And remember—your *past* in this case may have happened just yesterday. We often think of our memoirs as reflecting just our childhood or our young adult lives, but a memory of a striking event that occurred yesterday or last week will turn into one of those long-ago memories a few years from now.

The notes you've just made may look something like this:

> grandma's sugar cookies
> liver – forced to eat it
> mud pies

Now, take just one of your ideas, set a timer for 5 minutes, and write about that taste. When you experienced it, what it felt like in your mouth, who was with you at the time. Try to write for the full five minutes. That may seem like a long time, but if the timer is still ticking, you might think of some other aspect of your story that you can include.

When I conduct classes, I always ask after a writing exercise like this, "Does anyone want to share what you've written?"

Imagine you're in that class, and the person next to you raises their hand and reads: "I always hated eating asparagus, but my folks told me vegetables were important and I had to clean my plate, even though I gagged. They were tasteless, unless you can count all the salt."

"Did you dislike all vegetables, or only asparagus?" I ask.

15

Fran Stewart

"I liked peas and carrots."

"What did the asparagus look like?"

"It was limp and soggy."

"What a good description. Do you think you could include those words in your story? And tell us—was the asparagus fresh from the garden before it was cooked?"

"Heck no! It was always canned."

"Ah, I understand now. Can you see how that detail would add important information to help us visualize your story better?"

Another person speaks up and says, "I grew up on a farm. We always had fresh vegetables or ones we'd canned ourselves in glass Mason jars. I was twelve before I knew that other people had to eat food from tin cans."

"Great," I say. "That will be a story *you* can write. Years from now your grandchildren, who may very well live in a city, will get a much better idea of what growing up was like for you. And," I add, turning to the first writer, "*your* story may help someone understand how their own food aversions developed."

= = = = = = = = = =

Now, re-read what you've written about *your* particular taste and decide if you want to add some descriptive words or a few more details. Remember, the person reading your story may not know or recall the circumstances. If you're writing about your grandma's cookies, for instance – were they chocolate chip or sugar cookies, macaroons or pecan sandies? Were they moist and chewy or crisp and crackly? Did you help her bake them, or were they ready and waiting for you when you got home from school? Did she eat them along with you, or did she give you one and send you out to bring the garbage can up from the curb?

The good news about writing our stories is that we can always go back and fill in the details we may have missed the first time around.

= = = = = = = = = =

I hope you're ready to keep writing, because we still have four other senses to go. Pick the next one you have a specific memory about. **And please note the word *specific*.** A once-upon-a-time story isn't something like *I always loved the smell of new-mown grass*. You can start your story that way, but then give us the picture of a particular day, perhaps when you'd just ridden your bike home from a thoroughly discouraging soccer practice where you flubbed practically every kick you tried to make, and as soon as you turned the corner onto your street you could smell the grass cuttings wafting your way on the breeze. Tell us why that smell was important to you at the time. Who was doing the mowing – a parent, a neighbor, a teenager who'd started an after-school business? Did you love the smell because it meant the grass was already cut and you wouldn't have to ply the mower? Did the smell bring back memories of *another* day that was special to you?

And about that 5-minute timer I suggested: please don't think of it as limiting. If you're writing about how much the sound of your parents arguing in their bedroom late at night scared you, and that blinkin' timer goes off just as you're describing your fears, ignore the timer and keep on writing.

Before we go any further, I'd like to suggest that you consider asking a friend (or friends) to go through this process with you. You could meet in person or online to compare stories and discuss the progress you're making.

= = = = = = = = =

Now it's time for yet another sense-memory. Pick one of them and write about it. Or write another story about taste or smell or sound. Nothing says you have to stick with only one memory about each sense.

Over the course of this book, we'll talk about many other ways you can spice up your stories, but I'd like you to remember these sense-related exercises. You can always liven up your stories by including more sights, more sounds, more smells. Tell us how things felt when you touched them. Tell us how your mouth watered. Tell that special story that only you can tell.

Fran Stewart

Chapter 4 - The Other Senses

Now that you've written stories about sound and smell, touch and taste (and don't forget about sight), it's time to look at some of the other senses. At this point in my classes, I suggest one or two and then ask class members to add ones they might consider important. I usually start by mentioning:

> a sense of compassion and
> a sense of outrage

Some of the other senses contributed by class members are:

> delight / joy
> martyrdom
> optimism / pessimism
> empathy / sympathy
> justice
> entitlement
> loss / absence

You may very well have others you could add to the list. When you think of others, be sure to note them somewhere (here in the margins, the back of a used envelope, a pocket-sized notebook… The options are endless. Just be sure to remember where those notes are).

Now, let's consider these one at a time.

Compassion – When have you shown compassion to someone else, and did that action enrich your life? If so, in what way did you benefit? Was what you did appreciated or mistaken for pity?

On the other hand, when have you been the recipient of a compassionate act? What were the circumstances, and why was it important to you? Did that one act change your life in any way? If so, how?

Now there's the other side of the coin. Were there moments in your life when you cried out for compassion but did not receive it? When someone ignored your needs? Or – were there times when you feel you *could have / should have* shown compassion, but chose not to? How did these moments affect you? Every single one of these instances can provide the germ to start a story. *Once upon a time I …* Yes, that's how it starts.

Set your timer again (if that helps you) and answer these questions. Then go on to consider each of these others. If one doesn't ring a bell with you, that's okay. You can always return to that topic at a later date. Please use this book as a frequent resource, going back to review previous lessons and using them to encourage you to write more of your stories.

Sometimes we're not ready to deal with a particular issue. That doesn't mean you'll *never* be ready to write about it. Just maybe not right now.

Outrage – Most of us have felt outraged at one time or another. Explore the time(s) this happened in your life. Was your outrage justified? What action(s) did you take to express your anger? Or did you hold it all within until it spilled out at a later date? Keep in mind that outrage almost always erupts in one way or another. Did your outrage eat away at you? Or did you channel it into specific actions? What were the results? Did you try to understand (to have compassion for) the person who committed the outrage?

Some class members have asked how outrage differs from anger. A good question, indeed. *Anger* happens often; *outrage* is less common. Anger may be fairly minor – you're angry because somebody cut in line ahead of you or because someone borrowed your car and didn't fill the gas tank. Outrage, on the other hand, implies a much stronger emotion, because the reason for it generally breaks some sort of moral standard. We'll be angry about that empty gas tank but will feel outrage over a school shooting. Angry at seeing someone cheating on a high school history exam—thank goodness he was caught at it. But outraged when that person was inducted into the National Honor Society—that's a true story, based on my own life.

You're welcome, of course, to write about both anger and outrage. Just pick one and begin.

Keep in mind that when you include the lesson you learned from whatever happened to you, it can add an extra layer of value to your story.

That doesn't mean you have to sound like *Aesop's Fables* with a moral at the end of each! Sometimes a good story is just a good story:

How your mom thought your neck was dirty and scrubbed at what turned out to be the beginning of chicken pox, and you have the scars today to prove it—I did that to my son.

How you wrote a fascinating (you thought) letter to Santa Claus, sent it to the radio station to be read on the air, and then felt deflated when the announcer quoted two letters and then added, "Santa also got letters from Joe and Fran and Patty and Mario and Betsy." That's another personal memory of mine. I was dramatically disappointed, enough so that my mother ordered me to quit whining about it.

Delight / Joy – I've always felt a kinship with these words from William Wordsworth:

> My heart leaps up when I behold
> A rainbow in the sky…

Does that happen for you as well? The delight at seeing a rainbow (and particularly a double one!) never fades for me.

So, tell us – what brings you joy? What lifts your heart? Not just seeing any old rainbow, but seeing one, as I did, when my family was traveling through Germany on the way to my dad's latest assignment. There was a perfect double rainbow ahead of us, stretching all the way across the winding road. As my sister and I kept our eyes on it, the anticipation was delicious. Did it fade away? No. Did we drive right under it? Yes! Can I still feel the wind in my hair as I leaned out the car window (no seat belts in those days) to look upward hoping to see the underside of the arc? Yep. Will I remember that moment with great delight? Absolutely, no matter how many years have passed since it happened.

Set your timer now and write. Then come back for the next topic.

Martyrdom – I'm sure you've known a person (or two) against whom the world seems to hold a grudge. These are the people who see the storm cloud rather than the silver lining, the people who take umbrage at the slightest criticism, whether or not it was meant to be critical, the people you may feel you have to tiptoe around to keep from wounding them – although they seem easily wounded by *everything*.

Think about one of these people in your life and write about how their attitude affected you. Did you avoid that person or try to placate them? Did this result in long-term effects on your life? Were you ever able to develop a sense of compassion (there's that word again!) for this person, an understanding of how and why they became the way they were? Or do you still hold a grudge?

Optimism / Pessimism – Which is your general approach to life? How do you see current events? Do you surround yourself with like-minded people, or do you look to your friends to balance your view of life? Why do you feel your way of looking at things is best for you? Or *do* you consider it the best way? If not, how can you begin to revise your way of thinking?

Are there times when the other point of view is justified? Have you been criticized for being overly pessimistic – or overly optimistic?

You may think that this topic would be better off in a personal journal where you grapple with THE BIG PICTURE. The stories of your life, though, are a combination of what's happened to you *and* all the things you've thought about. People reading your stories years from now will appreciate the chance you've given them to look about inside your head.

During the COVID lock-down, I read through my grandfather's journals (1910-1967). When I got to his recounting of the flu pandemic during 1917 and 1918—the number of graves he had to dig, the uncertainty as to which neighbors were still alive—I realized how very fortunate I was. I had a phone, FaceTime, and Zoom so I could interact with friends and family. I went from feeling deprived to feeling blessed indeed.

Empathy / Sympathy – I'm sure you've heard of the difference between these two terms. Sympathy involves an understanding of what the other person is expressing, but empathy goes deeper, to where you *experience* what the other person is feeling. If a friend loses her father to cancer, you may feel a great deal of sympathy, but your response may not be truly empathetic unless you've also lost someone dear to you. So, let's explore those moments when you felt truly connected to someone else. Or have there been times when you benefitted from the empathy of a friend?

Have you ever felt empathy for a total stranger? Was it empathy or merely pity (which is a far-less-admirable version of sympathy)?

When I was a child, going to church when we visited my grandparents in a southern state, the hymns caused me physical pain. I've never been able to stand twangy, nasal singing, which is all that congregation was capable of. Of course, that was the way they'd been raised. That was what they were used to. And that was what they enjoyed. I held no understanding of their point of view. I was (silently) critical every time we entered that church. I *pitied* those people for not having the same appreciation for "good" music that I'd been trained to. I persisted in this attitude throughout a great deal of my adult life. But I had a wake-up moment a few years ago when a friend shared a video of her mother and grandmother singing (in another southern state), swaying back and forth to the raucous hymn, thoroughly enjoying themselves throughout the twangy tune. Admittedly, it wasn't my idea of beautiful music, but the joy was infectious.

There are countless ways you can approach an issue like this. Have you ever needed empathy from someone and were disappointed that they didn't seem to understand the depth of your sorrow? I once shared a story about something devastating that had happened to me as a child, and the person I told it to, obviously overwhelmed by what I'd said, told me, "That was a long time ago. Get over it." Neither sympathetic nor empathetic.

Or have you tried to share the way joy welled up in you after a particular achievement? Did they celebrate with you or were they just waiting anxiously to relate their own accomplishments?

If you've had such moments, writing about how they affected you will make a good *once-upon-a-time*. The people who read your story years from now may be inspired to consider their own reactions to tragedy or exhilaration in others, to consider how a shift in their point of view can affect their entire life.

Justice – Here's a sense that may or may not be closely related to the sense of outrage we discussed earlier, for when justice is denied we may become highly incensed. Sometimes though, it's just a matter of whether or not the books of life are in balance. We see this a lot in children, most of whom have a finely tuned perception of what's right and what's wrong, at least in their young world. Bullying on the playground is bad. Sharing is good. Holding hands when you cross the street is right. Lying to your friends is wrong. Children know what's fair and what isn't.

Think about times in your life when your sense of justice was either confirmed or offended. Remember that years from now, social mores may have shifted in such a way that what seems outrageous now is acceptable then. Or vice versa.

Tell your stories about the times you've been angered over a lack of justice, or when you've felt satisfied that justice has been well-served.

Entitlement – There's a great deal of talk nowadays about how many people feel a sense of entitlement—an expectation that life will give them everything they deserve (or think they do).

When have you felt entitled to something? Were your expectations fulfilled or disappointed?

Was your sense of entitlement the result of receiving too many accolades for mediocre achievements? Or from not getting the attention or acknowledgement you thought you deserved?

In one of the classes I taught, a woman said she was the youngest of seven children. All her older sisters and brothers excelled at sports—tennis, football, lacrosse, gymnastics…. When she finally won a red ribbon for coming in second in a relay race, several of her sibs made fun of her and showed off their first- and second-place trophies. Was she angry with her sibs because of their teasing? No. She was angry with the coach of her track team for not having a trophy available.

When she shared this memory in class, I was reminded of a story I'd written some time ago. When my children were young, they brought home the most garish trophies for practically every event they competed in. First, second, third place—it didn't matter. They got a trophy for it. Over the years the trophies accumulated. Eventually when we faced a move, I asked how many of the trophies meant a lot to them. It turns out, none of them did.

I, on the other hand, still have the awards I won for speech competitions when I was a senior in high school back in the 60s. My dad was stationed at Scott Air Base in Illinois, which meant that I attended a small near-by town school. Mrs. Van Aken, the English and Speech teacher, was superb. She insisted on absolute excellence in every poem we recited, every story we read aloud, every debate issue we advanced. Toward the end of that year, the Illinois State Speech Association sponsored a state-wide speech contest. I was entered in the poetry division, reading selections from *Spoon River Anthology* by Edgar Lee Masters, a collection of epitaphs spoken by the inhabitants of the fictional Spoon River cemetery.

We first competed within our school district, then the winners went on to a regional competition. Over the course of these contests, I competed against hundreds of other participants.

Eventually, the finalists of each regional contest competed at the state level. Our little delegation was up against the BIG schools—Chicago, Champlain-Urbana, Springfield, Bloomington-Normal, and Peoria. We were judged multiple times by various English/Speech professionals, and when the final scores were computed, I came out as number 1 verse reader in the entire state, which meant I then had to perform in front of the hundreds of people who had attended this three-day event—contestants, coaches, family members, staff people, and all the judges for each category. The auditorium was packed.

I ended my recitation by quoting from Edgar Lee Masters' own epitaph:

> Good friends, let's to the fields.
> I have a fever.
> After a little walk, and by your pardon,
> I think I'll sleep. There is no sweeter thing
> Nor fate more blessed than to sleep.
> Here, world. I pass you
> Like an orange to a child.
> I can no more with you.
> Do what you will.

Now, what's the point of all this? When the awards were presented onstage in the huge auditorium, I received an oval gold-colored medal (1¼ inches high by 1 inch wide) that features the IHSA logo. It hangs from a gold-colored bar (1½ inches wide by ¼ inch high) that says simply *State Championship*. To this day I treasure it, as I treasure my memories of finding the bravery to speak before such intimidating audiences. Did I need a two-foot-tall trophy? No. The little medal is more than enough.

Now, if this story were all I'd written about in my memoirs, it wouldn't really be enough. I needed to balance it with the story of how, in college, I was entered in a "persuasive speech" competition. Why my professor ever let me enter, I have no idea. My speech was truly horrible. Knowing how badly I'd performed in one of the rounds, I left the stage to rejoin my friends in the audience and gave them an apologetic smile before I sat down, fully cognizant that I'd let down the whole team with my poor showing. On the judging sheet I received afterwards, one of the judges had written his scathing review and then added, "And that self-satisfied smirk you gave before you sat down was completely unjustified."

Fran Stewart

So, when you write your stories, be willing to make yourself vulnerable. Be willing to expose the mistakes you've made, the times your judgment was less than acute, the times you should have done something and didn't (or *shouldn't* have done something but did).

And to go back for a moment to the Masters epitaph, this brings to mind what we face in writing our stories.

> Here, world. I pass you
> Like an orange to a child.
> I can no more with you.
> Do what you will.

We have no idea how our descendants will treat our stories—whether they will treasure them or discount them or disagree with them or simply love them. Their reaction isn't the point of all this. You'll be leaving your mark on the world, recalling the times / events that were important to you. What the people hereafter do with them is not up to us. And that's okay.

Before we go on to the final topic in this chapter, let me emphasize that the length of your stories is not all that important. Compare my short rainbow memory with the long speech-award one. The length isn't as important as the content. As you write your stories don't concentrate so much on how long they are (or aren't). Instead, try to infuse them with the specific details that will allow your readers to feel they're with you no matter where you're going in your story.

Remember, the way you tell your story will be so much more powerful if your reader can not only see what you're seeing but can feel what you're feeling.

Loss – Aah. One of the hardest topics for many people to write about. And yet loss is something that occurs to each of us countless times over the course of our lives. It may be something as *simple* as losing our way to or from an important meeting (my sister always told me I could get lost in a phone booth—thank goodness for GPS navigation), or as *heart-wrenching* as the loss of a child, which I've never experienced myself, but I've had friends who *have* lost children either to accident, still birth, or disease.

Back in the 1980s, when my children were in grade school, the school librarian lost her daughter to cancer. I didn't know her well, but wanted to send a sympathy card, and I recalled a story I'd read somewhere or other. So I wrote it out onto a notecard, and mailed it to her. Here's the story:

> I am standing on the seashore. A ship at the pier spreads her white sails to the morning breeze and heads for the wide blue ocean. She is magnificent, full of beauty and strength. I stand and watch her until she finally hangs like a speck of white cloud just where the sea and sky come together.
>
> Then someone at my side sobs and says, "Oh no! She is gone!"
>
> "Gone?" I question. "She isn't gone. Gone perhaps from our sight, but still there. Her sails still billow in the wind, and her keel is still as strong against the waters of the ocean as when she left us. Her cargo is still safe.
>
> "Her diminished size is in *me*, not in *her*. And I know full well that somewhere on a far shore, someone sees the approaching sail, and while you are saying *she is gone*, the ones there are giving a glad shout: *Look! She comes!*"

Eleven years after I sent the school librarian that card, I moved to Georgia.

Several years after THAT, I got a card in the mail from someone with a Vermont return address. I didn't recognize the name.

Inside was a hand-written note thanking me for the story about the ship that I had written to her so many years before. "Since then," she told me, "I have known four other people who've lost children, and I've copied that story for each one of them. Thank you from the bottom of my heart for having given me such a gift that I could share with others who needed it."

Ironically, a few years later, when my dad was dying, I found the same story on the last page of a booklet about dying that the hospice nurse gave us.

Did you notice that I hadn't even remembered writing that original card, until I received the librarian's note? Our acts of generosity may be forgotten, either by ourselves or by others, but if we've written about them, they'll continue to live on. And what we write now may

Fran Stewart

persuade future readers to perform their own acts of generosity.

= = = = = = = = = = = = = =

I hope you've been inspired to write a whole slew of your stories. Even if you've written only one or two, please don't feel discouraged. You can do this. It's just a matter of thinking about each of the topics I've introduced, combing your memories, and then sitting down with paper and pencil (or computer), and recording your words.

Speaking of recording, one of the younger people who took an in-person class said that her children would never sit down and read written words. "Neither of them likes to read. Period. They'll listen to audio books or read texts, but that's about it."

"That's okay," I told her. "Why don't you record your stories and save them that way?"

"That'll work!" She left the class in a much better mood.

As with each of these lessons, if you have questions or concerns, you're welcome to contact me through my website at franstewart.com/ contact .

Chapter 5 - Prompts

Now that you've explored the world of the senses, let's move on to some other ways to get you writing more of your life stories. One of the easiest ways is to listen to the prompts around you.

"What the heck is a prompt?"

I'm glad you asked.

Simply stated, a prompt is *any word or phrase that triggers a memory about a story you'd like to tell.*

Think back to Chapter 3 when one woman described how she hated everything about asparagus and another woman in the class remembered the fresh asparagus from her childhood on a farm. She had her own story to tell about fresh veggies. In this case, the words *canned asparagus* served as a prompt to tweak the second woman's memory about something she'd taken very much for granted—the vibrant taste of fresh-grown anything.

She might not have thought her experience was all that interesting, but to someone reading about the way she and her mother dug an asparagus bed, planted the crowns, tended them carefully, and waited the three to five years for the first harvest—can you see how that would be an eye-opener for a city-bred individual? Or maybe the prompt triggered a memory of pulling up carrot sprouts to see if the bright orange veggie had developed yet—and learning her lesson that patience was a requirement when growing a garden. The story I wrote after that class about my own asparagus bed involved telling how I dug the 12" deep trench and planted my first asparagus crowns when I was six months pregnant with my second child. Just as the first spears were ready for harvest, we moved to another house and the new owners benefited from my endeavors.

So, any time you hear a passing comment from someone—from anyone whether you know them or not—if a word or two catches your attention, jot it down somewhere (You *do* have a notebook with you all the time, don't you? Or a phone you can keep notes on?). This way you can return to your list of prompts at a later date. They'll jog your memory so you write that story you might not have remembered to write otherwise.

Let me give you a few examples of prompts I've responded to over the years:

Kitchen counters

       Wrinkles
       Hitting bottom
       Old photographs
       Bad medical advice

And here are some other prompt suggestions that have come from class members:

       Mountain climbing
       Disaster vacation
       Reading
       Curiosity
       Favorite teacher
       Laughter
       Trampolines
       Graduation
       Greece

For each of these, you may not have a memory of your own, or your memory may be slightly different, just as someone may hear *asparagus* and write about carrots instead. The *wrinkles* you write about may be your own or they may be your grandmother's; the *mountain* you write about may be a physical mountain you climbed or a seemingly insurmountable difficulty you faced or are facing.

The *trampoline* idea may suggest either a childhood memory or the concept of wondering why you always seem to bounce from one project to another without truly finishing any of them. How many unfinished crochet / knitting / embroidery projects do I have in my sewing box?

Thinking about *medical advice* may prompt you to write about how you barely survived a rare disease that took years to be diagnosed properly. Or it may encourage you to write about the lack of adequate nearby healthcare in the village where you grew up, and *that* may have prompted you to establish a health clinic in that same village.

Hearing someone refer to *Greece* may prompt you to write about backpacking through Switzerland or going on a camera safari in Kenya. By the same token, it might remind you of a time when you spilled hot *grease* from a pan over your gas stove and started a raging house fire.

As you can see, the actual wording of the prompt is secondary to the idea it sparks within you. Once you feel that spark, you can start writing. Let's do that now. Take one of these prompts and expand on it any way that seems right to you. Try to use *sense* words or ideas. Be sure to incorporate *specifics* rather than just talking in generalities. Where were you when this happened? How old were you? Who was with you? How did you feel at the time? What was the result? Did it change your life in any way?

Okay? Set your timer (optional) and try to write for at least five minutes.

After you've written your prompted memory, re-read it (aloud if possible) and think of ways you can spice up the story, maybe by adding more details here and there.

= = = = = = = = = = = = = =

Next, write a simple remembrance from your own life about one of the following three prompts:

> Unexpected event. This can be a car wreck or a pee-in-my-pants moment or forgetting your sister's name
> First job. Either as a child, a teenager, or an adult
> A reason to smile. Of course, that reason can be either ironic or actual

After you've written it, go through the same routine of reading what you wrote, listening to yourself read it—do the words flow easily, or have you tried to be pretentious? Remember, somebody else will be reading these stories of yours in the future, and they're more likely to continue to read them if you say:

When I broke my leg, the cast was so heavy I had to hobble around for a couple of months,

rather than:

Perambulation was extremely difficult after I sustained an injury involving a fracture to my femur.

If it helps, imagine yourself and some friends sitting around a campfire trading stories. If you're not the outdoorsy type, see yourself sitting across from someone at a cozy kitchen table with tea or coffee or cocoa (or anything else) between you. Whatever you can imagine to help you tell your stories is the perfect way for *you*.

And, just for the fun of it, here's a list of the prompts that came from a couple of recent classes:

Cartoons
Shock
Valentine's card
Gardening
His smile
Scotch
Evening gown
Whales
Belly laughs
Inner tubes
Spud (my dog)
Ocean
Gramophone
Bears

Another prompt was *favorite song* – and a reminder about this one: while it's tempting to assume that a song we love will be remembered for generations, that's not always the case. You might want to do a search for the lyrics online. Copy and paste them into your story if you think that will help future readers.

Now pick one or two or three of these topics. Write!

Chapter 6 – The Importance of Perspective

A number of years ago, I found a picture online that made me stop and wonder just how awful the "poet" must be. How could anyone have such a negative view of life in general and of art in particular?

But then I read further and found the true story.

First let me explain that I contacted the artist, **Jasmine Kay**, and asked for her permission (which I received) to use her work in my memoirs classes.

Imagine that you're entering the Art Building at your university. As you step out of the bright sunshine, you're confronted with a wide column that stretches from the floor almost to the ceiling. It's an art installation that Ms. Kay created. You stop to read the words:

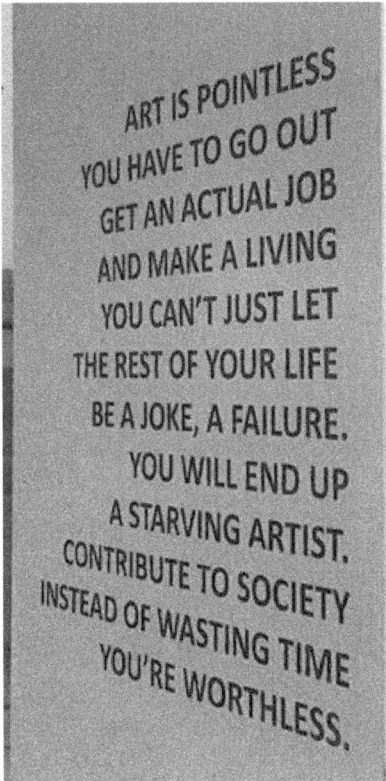

ART IS POINTLESS
YOU HAVE TO GO OUT
GET AN ACTUAL JOB
AND MAKE A LIVING
YOU CAN'T JUST LET
THE REST OF YOUR LIFE
BE A JOKE, A FAILURE.
YOU WILL END UP
A STARVING ARTIST.
CONTRIBUTE TO SOCIETY
INSTEAD OF WASTING TIME
YOU'RE WORTHLESS.

Pointless??? How terrible is that? How very soul crushing for someone who is yet unsure about their art and the place for their talents in society. You begin to wonder who you can complain to about this horrible exhibit. Where did this come from, anyway? And what's it doing in a place that's supposed to encourage artistic endeavors?

Now, walk a little farther around to your right to reach the stairs behind the column.

Ahh! Now you can see the second side of the column and can read the poetic essay in its entirety. "Art is pointless without passion." Keep reading…

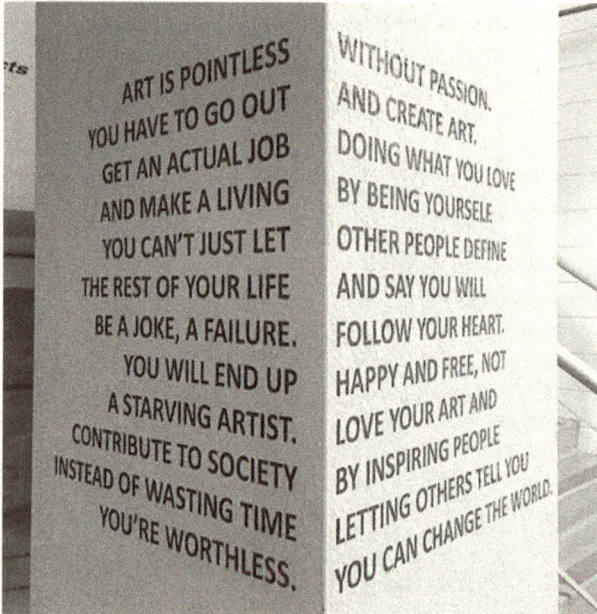

Now you've gained a sense of perspective, a chance to see something disturbing from a different point of view. Now you can see the value in the big picture.

How often in life, though, do we forget to take those few steps forward? How often do we not realize there's another side to be seen? How often are we trapped in preconceived notions that no longer serve us?

I'll give you a couple of examples from my own life of how this can happen. The first one I've never shared with any of my classes because it happened to me only last night (just when I needed it for this chapter!)

I have a strange sleeping pattern. I tend to wake in the middle of almost every night and spend an hour or two with my eyes wide open. I've learned to turn on a light and use the time to read, to jot down book ideas, to work diagramless or jigsaw-sudoku or crossword puzzles (thanks to Penny Dell Puzzles, from whom I order on a regular basis).

Sometimes I step out onto my front porch and refill the bird feeder there.

Yes, I use the time productively, but I've always considered it a *wasted* time. A time when I should be sleeping. A time that's all out of sorts. Despite the fact that I learned that this was a regular sleep pattern for most people before the eternal lights of the Industrial Revolution threw off any sort of universal sleep patterns. The French had a term for this. They called this wakefulness *dorveille*, followed by what they termed the *second sleep*. All very primeval, very normal, right? But I still felt out of sorts, still felt it was somehow wrong.

This morning, though, I stepped onto my porch, birdseed and dried mealworms in hand, and drank in the soft, misty, rain-laden darkness. The quiet. The peacefulness of it all, and I called up from some strange recess within me a poem I learned back in college – *Hymn to the Night* by Henry Wadsworth Longfellow. The part I recalled so early this morning was:

> O holy Night! From thee I learn to bear
> What man has borne before!
> Thou layest thy finger on the lips of Care,
> And they complain no more.

I'm not going to resent my *dorveille* anymore. That resentment was the left-hand side of the column. I'm going to use it well by stepping around to the other side of that column. Then I'll be able to welcome my second sleep with open arms and a peaceful heart.

Now for the second story from my own experience. Like many of our life stories, it requires a bit of background before you can appreciate it (since you weren't there). Go back to Chapter 4 where we talked about the *other senses*. Remember the sense of martyrdom? Here's my very personal story. It happened in my childhood and affected me for more years than I care to admit.

The first view of this column in my life happened when I was five. My mother was one of the unhappiest people I've ever known. She was the epitome of martyrdom. She spent her whole life hoping somehow that other people could fill the gulf of emptiness within her, but of course that could never happen. When I was five, I didn't understand any of this. I didn't know how undiagnosed clinical depression could color a person's entire life. Nor did I know how an abused child often carried the emotional scars into the rest of her life. All I knew was that it was never safe to tell my mother how I really felt about anything she did.

My sister was four years older than I, and she'd reached that stage of her life where sexual exploration was a normal part of her development. I wasn't at that stage yet, and I hated the fact that I had to be her "patient" when she wanted to play "doctor."

Our mother caught us one day and went absolutely ballistic. I'm surprised I don't still bear *physical* scars from her explosive anger – but I did for many years bear the *emotional* scars of the terror I endured over not just the physical agony but from the words of loathing she screamed at me.

At that time, my five-year-old self decided that
      1) I was worthless,
      2) People I trusted would always hurt me, and
      3) I had no real control over what happened in my life.

That was my view of the first side of the column, and I maintained that subconscious mindset well into my adult life. It took years of counseling, workshops, and forgiveness exercises for me to step around to the second side and to understand my mother's wounds—the depression, the abuse she'd suffered at the hands of her father and her uncle, the way she was unable *ever* to forgive anyone for anything, even if the slight was just something she imagined.

But I finally, in my late forties, succeeded in true forgiveness, in letting go of the burden of resentment I'd carried around on my back like a misguided Santa.

That forgiveness (which by the way did not mean that what she had done was okay, but rather that I'd released the ties of anger that chained me to her long-ago actions)—forgiving her meant that when she finally died, there were only the two of us in the room: my mother and me. There wasn't any anger, resentment, fear, distrust, dislike, anguish, terror. All of that was gone.

For years my mother's arthritic hands had been gnarled almost completely shut. But when she died, I saw the moment that elusive breath of life left her body, and at that very moment, her clenched hands relaxed. Her congestive heart condition didn't matter anymore. Her dementia was a thing of the past.

A year later, I wrote a poem that has become one of my "life stories," in that it tells not only precisely what happened that night, but also the lesson I learned from it.

Resolution
a poem in 3-3-5-9 meter
© *2004 Fran Stewart*

The night my mother died
I sang and read and prayed.
I knitted as I thought about my life
And saw the fraying strands that joined me with that
woman lying on the bed.

The night my mother died
I listened to her breathe,
Then set aside my knitting and my book.
I called my sister, moved my chair across the room, up to
my mother's bed.

I took her hand in mine
And eased my other hand,
Light as I could, straight on her struggling heart.
So frail—the fluttering of a dozen finches brushed against
my fingertips.

The night my mother died
I held her crumpled hand,
No stranger—that—to me. I recognized
Her fingers—gnarled, tight-jointed, twisted, frozen in an
agonized refrain.

I worked my fingers in.
Her fist was closed. So tight.

So barricaded, as her heart had been.
The clock above her bed struck one. The finches shook.
Her breath was hard to hear.

And when my mother died,
She took a final breath.
She held it, arched her back and groaned, and then
She sang her final song, a long slow sigh that lifted her,
and she was gone.

The finches hadn't heard.
For ninety years they'd beat
Their wings, for ninety seconds more they tried.
They fluttered, faltered, strove to fly, and settled, finally,
folding in their wings.

The night my mother died,
Her hand, so tight, so closed,
Opened, and I held a baby's hand,
Soft and supple. Liver-spotted, yes. But—somehow—
new.

The gift my mother gave
To me the night she died
Was a deep, strong, heart-committed knowing
That I will never close my fist and wait for Death to come
and open it.

At this point you may be wondering "Why on earth would Fran openly share such embarrassing stories?"

That's a good question.

The answer is that I've discovered over the years of teaching these classes that when I'm willing to make myself vulnerable, it opens a pathway for others to address the hidden parts of their own lives. They may choose—and *you* may choose—not to share such moments in your own life, but if you *do* share them, you may find that others will say, "I thought I was the only one," or "Now I get what was going on when I went through the same sort of thing."

When I moved to Georgia in the early 1990s, I was able to reconnect with my mother's younger sister, an aunt I hadn't seen since my childhood. "Your mother always volunteered to go with Uncle Joe or with Daddy," she said. "She did it to protect us younger girls so we wouldn't have to go through what she went through." It took me a long time to digest that piece of the puzzle, but it was one more step toward my seeing the whole picture of why my mother was the way she was—toward my getting a true sense of perspective.

Now, it's time for you to think of a way in which your perspective has changed over the past years (or months or days, even). It doesn't have to be anything dramatic like my second story.

It could be something gentle, the way I woke up to realizing my wakefulness wasn't worthy of resentment.

It could be finally understanding how a disappointment you experienced long ago led you to a new determination and took your life in an unexpected direction.

It may be learning that the child you thought made a miserable showing in a piano recital had a learning disability that meant what he accomplished in the recital was a hallmark of true progress—which helped you understand the senselessness of making judgments without having the proper knowledge.

Set your timer and write about that change in your life—what the background was, how you came to a new realization, what you learned from it, how it made your life better.

And if you want to pursue this further, go back to the past exercises we've done and see if you might want to revise some of what you've written with this new sense of perspective in mind.

Here's one more thing to think about: It's important to date your stories. The reason? Something you write today may reflect a point of view that you may change in ten years—or ten weeks—or even ten days. So, when you write that second story to show how your thinking has involved, the people coming after you will be able to tell how quickly (or not-so-quickly) your thoughts progressed.

Fran Stewart

Chapter 7 – What About Family Secrets?

This is a question I get asked a lot, usually in a whispered tête-a- tête after everyone else has left the classroom, or in a private email. Nobody has ever asked it aloud where others could hear.

What's so secret about family secrets? The answer may seem incredibly obvious: *Duh! It's a secret.* Well, yes, but there's an aspect to that secrecy that needs to be addressed. In my book *After I Die: What My Executor Will Need to Know* I address that very issue this way:

> If you have secrets, as most people do, rest
> assured that they are likely to be uncovered at
> some point after your death. There is space in
> any life for <u>privacy</u>, but <u>secrets</u> tend to be toxic
> and may bring pain to your survivors.
>
> You might want to consider these four
> things now:
>
> o   What those secrets are
> o   What disruption their discovery will cause
> o   What to do about revealing them before
>   you die, or
> o   How to leave an explanation so your
>   family isn't torn apart. As I say, this is
>   just something for you to think about.

One of the family secrets several different class members shared with me was the existence of another family, complete with children, living in another town or another state. One wife found out when the *other* wife showed up at the funeral. The other case was revealed when an unknown daughter wrote on the funeral home's online obituary that her father had been a focal point in her life, even though his work meant he was gone so often. Of course he was gone. That was when he was staying with his other family.

This situation brought up real problems for each executor. Which was the legal marriage? What was the validity of each will if there were two documents with conflicting information? What if one family had a will and the other one didn't?

My father once killed a man. It was an accident, when a barroom brawl went awry, and the man my father punched fell backwards onto a sharp table corner and split his head wide open. My dad was only 18 at the time and roaming the country as a hobo during the Great Depression. He and his hobo buddies jumped onto a boxcar headed out of the state and got away from the mob chasing them.

He never told anyone about this until he was close to dying himself. Did telling us make a difference to the man who died? No. Or to that unknown man's family? No. But it lifted a load off my father's shoulders that he'd carried for more than 70 years.

Do you have a secret you've been carrying?

Not every family secret need be as dramatic as these situations. It can be a jail sentence that you never told anyone about, a drug or alcohol addiction you overcame, a petty crime that you never reported, a youthful joyride that went horribly wrong. It can be a name change, a cruel act of some sort that you never apologized for. In fact, it can be just about anything that you don't want anybody to know about.

But, trust me, it probably will come to light somehow or other. Even if it might not, do you really want to take the chance?

Now is the time for you to consider those four items I mentioned earlier. I would assume you don't want your family torn apart. You can do something now to keep that from happening.

Do you need to apologize for something? If so, be sure to consider that step in AA that says something like "make amends to people, but only if doing so will not harm them or others."

And you'll want to take care of yourself, so consider your options, which may involve counseling before you do any apologizing.

Other things to think about:

> How serious was the event you have hidden?
> Were you the perpetrator or the victim?
> Be as open and honest as you can.

And if you decide to share your story, choose your confidante very carefully. That person may not want to hear what you have to say. My daughter, for instance, reacted negatively when I told her about the abuse from my mother. "I want to love Grandma," she said. "I don't want to hear anything bad about her." My telling her, though, did let her understand why I had always refused to let my parents take my children on extended vacations.

Now's the time for you to think about all this. Do something. Write about your decision.

You are also welcome to share your secret with me, knowing that I will respect your confidence and will delete your email after I read it. If you want me to respond to you, I will. Just let me know your wishes (franstewart.com/contact).

A Footnote:

And then there are the private issues—the ones that might not be at the *secret* level, but are still potentially embarrassing, or that simply show you in a less-than favorable light. This brings us back to that idea of being willing to make yourself vulnerable.

Remember that what you write today may well provide a roadmap for someone in the future. They can learn from your mistakes. They can come to admire your bravery in admitting them.

Now's the time to think about all this. And then to write.

Fran Stewart

Chapter 8 – How to Handle Your Stories

This is another topic I'm asked about at every single class I teach. There are two very different aspects of this issue. The first is how to keep track of what you've written. The second is how to organize the stories within that tracking system.

Let's address the first question first.

How to keep track of your stories.
This isn't a particularly vital question if you have only three or four or even twenty stories. You'll be able to remember what they are and where you put them. The issue becomes much more important, though, once you've amassed a wealth of stories. So here are four good ideas:

> How about just writing everything in a **notebook**? Your own handwriting will add a flair to this process. I picture my father distinctly every time I see his handwriting. But here's a potential problem: can your grandchildren read cursive?

> **File folders** are good if you want to reorganize the order of your stories. Write each story separately and then stick them in the file folder.

> Many people prefer to write their stories on their **computer,** which is great as long as it doesn't crash. Be sure to have an external backup – or keep printed copies of each story.

> This leads us to the idea of **3-ring binders**, which will work with either printed or handwritten stories, particularly if you use some sort of dividers to separate your stories into categories, which is a good segue into the idea of…

Organizing your stories into categories
First, be sure the title says what the story is. Something like *A Childhood Memory* is no help whatsoever if you're trying to find the one about when the emu chased you at the petting zoo. Solve this by putting *Emu* in that title!

Organizing isn't usually possible if you're writing your stories, one after the other, into a notebook. But all three of the other systems

Fran Stewart

(folders, computer, or binders) can benefit from having the stories grouped into some sort of logical sequence. Here are four possibilities:

> **Chronological** – You can group your stories by year / by school grade / by age group (child / school / teen / adult / middle age / retirement). Put them into separate file folders (keeping them in one of those milk-crate containers), store them in different sub-folders on your computer (all grouped, of course, under one main folder called *Memoirs*), or arrange them in your 3-ring binder separated by colorful dividers.
>
> You may choose instead to group your stories by **Theme**. These could be something like lessons I've learned / people I've known / jobs I've had.
>
> One woman who took my class said she wanted to group all her stories by the **Senses** we talked about in Chapter 3. She was going to write lots of stories about sights she'd seen (she'd traveled through four of the continents), tastes she'd experienced (she'd eaten all the local cuisines), sounds she'd heard (from the laughter of children to the screams in a marketplace after a terrorist bombing). And so on. Although I must admit I didn't see how that type of story classification could possibly work, I encouraged her to go for it. "No matter how you start," I told the entire class, "you can always change your system at a later date."
>
> You may want to group your stories into sections of **Contrasts**, a happy story followed by a sad one / one that shows how smart you were followed by one that shows how incredibly dumb you've been.

The way you organize them may not make sense to anyone else—but if it makes sense to you, that's what counts.

And it just occurred to me that this will work even for notebook writers. Have one notebook for each category!

You might want to include a section somewhere or other about stories you've heard, but didn't directly experience, such as the tales about your great-grandfather who settled out West before there were states there, or the grandmother who chased a bull that had jumped over the fence from a neighboring farm—and lived to tell about it.

All right—there's one more way of organizing. I call this the **Mishmash** approach. It fits perfectly into writing everything in a notebook. One person who took my class brought his laptop to each session. When we talked about organizing the stories, he turned the laptop around so we could see that each story he'd written was a Word document he'd saved on his desktop. The screen was *filled* with little rectangular icons, many of which had nothing to do with his memoirs. They were all jumbled together.

I was appalled. What will happen, I wondered, when there's no more room on his screen? But he was comfortable with it, so it didn't really matter what I thought.

If you haven't written enough stories yet to worry about organization, don't be concerned. You can always come back to this chapter at a later date. But you might want to keep some of these ideas in mind before your stories become too numerous.

Fran Stewart

Chapter 9 – Buckets

I'd like us to spend a little time considering a favorite quotation of mine. It's from Mary Webb (1881-1927) who wrote:

> "The Well of Providence is deep. It's the buckets we
> bring to it that are small."

Think about it. We are surrounded, always, whether or not we're aware of it, by miracles. Tiny flowering weeds growing up between sidewalk squares. Lichen on tree trunks. The beating hearts of those we love. Stars at night. Laughter. Birds and squirrels in city parks. Music. Precious animal companions. The occasional rainbow. Life itself.

Even if the power grid fails, these miracles will persist. These gifts that we haven't even asked for are abundant. They are great. We have only to recognize them in order to fill our "buckets" with the largesse of the world. But every time we fail to see the specialness of life, we are in effect bringing extremely small buckets to that well of providence.

I'd like you to think about each of these small miracles I've listed. Pick one or two of them (or more!) and spend a few moments writing about when you were last aware—not only aware, but appreciative— of them. If none of these seem to speak to you, find some other small miracles in your daily routine and write about them. What you write now may help someone in the future wake up to an awareness of life that they've been missing.

Now consider this question: Where in your life do you use *small* buckets? Have you ignored the kindness of a friend (or a complete stranger)? When you're cozy inside during a rainstorm, do you gaze out the window and see the beauty of it all? Have you turned your back on a chance to help people less fortunate than yourself? Have you let fear (**F**alse **E**vents **A**ppearing **R**eal) stop you from reaching for something you'd like to accomplish—a better job, a better relationship, a wider audience for your ideas, an invention you have in mind, a scholarship you'd like to found, a child you'd like to foster, a song you'd like to write?

When you've finished writing about these things, you just might find a larger bucket to carry around with you every day. Sure would be a good idea!

My friend Marcia told me a favorite "bucket" story of hers and reminded me that we sometimes limit our prosperity. Here's her story: A woman camping by a small lake went fishing. She kept only the small ones and threw back all the larger ones. Why? Her cast iron camping skillet was fairly small, and the longer fish wouldn't fit. Don't have a small bucket? Maybe you have a small skillet...

Chapter 10 – Choosing the Right Details

We've already talked about choosing interesting details to make our stories more vibrant. Including sense images, for instance, can help those reading your stories feel they're right there with you. Colors, sounds, tastes (even though describing a taste can be challenging; try saying how the taste affected you. Were you intrigued by it or revolted?) Each of these will add an immediacy to the story you're telling.

You can avoid the too-common descriptives such as *little, big, awful, happy,* or *sad* by doing a global search for each of those words and then replacing them judiciously.

Little: was something miniscule or just hard-to-spot among the larger items? **Big**: was it heavy (like an unabridged dictionary) or mountainous (like a national monument)? **Awful**: was it filthy, revolting, or simply ugly?   **Happy**: were you exhilarated or simply contented? **Sad**: downhearted or inconsolable?

If you find yourself writing that you were ***scared***, stop and consider that word. Were you truly terrified by what had just happened to you, or were you merely startled?

Or let's say you're writing about people you've met throughout your extensive travels. If you describe each one of them as ***amazing***, can you see how that adjective might seem a bit stale after one or two? One of these people might have astonished you, while another stupefied you. One might have inspired awe and another seemed more sensational. This woman may have created a remarkable home industry in an area with poor natural resources, and a different woman might have flabbergasted you with her willingness to confront authority. All of these people were amazing, but that word weakens with each repetition.

There's yet another aspect to the selection of an apt descriptive word or phrase. We can sway the opinion of our readers in such a subtle way that they might not even realize they're being pointed in a particular direction. People who write should always be aware of the final result of their words. I find it interesting to look at the way newspaper articles or blog posts are worded. This kind of manipulation is sometimes so subtle as to be nearly indistinguishable from "just-the-facts" reporting (or story-telling).

What am I talking about? Here are some examples. Look at each way of expressing these events and see how changing a word or two here and there can completely reverse your reader's (and your own) perception of the event.

Describing a crowd at a public event you attended:

Almost a hundred people gathered to hear so-and-so, even though *it rained heavily.*

Not even a hundred people showed up to hear so-and-so *in the rain*, even though *there wasn't any lightning or thunder*.

On the surface, each of these statements is true, but look more closely at the final picture each presents. The first sounds like you were glad you were there with all those other like-minded people, doesn't it? The second expresses your vague disappointment in the low turnout.

Describing last night's sleep:

I *tossed and turned* before I *made it to sleep.*

I *wiggled and snuggled* before I *slipped into dreamland.*

Okay, maybe example #2 is a bit schmaltzy, but it certainly sounds like you had a better night than the one in the sentence before the snuggling.

Describing the ring of a phone:

When it *broke into my consciousness* I *groped for the doggone thing*.

When it *chimed,* I *answered happily.*

These two examples don't express whether you were wakened from a deep sleep or interrupted in the middle of a vital task, but the first clearly expresses anger (or at least irritation), while the second shows your delight. You'll have to let us know in the rest of that story whether you knew who was calling or why you were either glad or irritated when you were interrupted.

If you'd like another example, here's a story I wrote in 2006 after a somewhat humbling evening when I spoke to a book club about my second mystery. The third one had just been released. I was still at that new-author stage of thinking that everyone would obviously love (and would buy) my books. As you read, see if you can figure out just from my word choices whether my mood was primarily positive or mostly negative.

Lesson in Humility

Last night I loaded 42 books in my truck and drove 35 miles in a blinding rainstorm to a book club meeting. The hostess had told me that there would be twenty-two women, all of whom had thoroughly enjoyed reading *Yellow as Legal Pads*. She served wine, and by the time we were halfway through the evening, three of the fourteen women there were schnockered and two others went to sleep sitting up. *Guess I'm not as popular as I thought I was*, I mused.

One woman proclaimed loudly that she had "bought a used copy of *Yellow* on Amazon." She paused for effect. "Cheap!" she added. As the other women congratulated her on her bargain, I even managed to nod my head, without gritting my teeth.

Three of the women had borrowed the book from someone else. Five told me they hadn't read the book because it wasn't in the library. One woman complained because I had killed off "such a nice hunk." Bull Finney? Nice? "Prove to me that he wasn't a nice guy," she challenged. So I read her the section where Linda thinks about the nasty way he had of undercutting her in front of their kids, and the one about how he lied about being a blood donor. My challenger crossed her arms. She was not convinced.

The customer is always right. Remember that, Frannie.

When I showed them my latest book, *Green as a Garden Hose*, one of the women declared that she liked only short books. *Green* was way too thick for her even to consider reading.

"Did you like the Book Club Discussion Questions for *Yellow*?" I asked the group in some desperation.

"No," they sang out, almost like a chorus line. "I never read those things." "I used to be a counselor; I don't need anybody to think up questions for me." "Are you kidding? We have *you* here. Why should we read questions?"

After the last woman left, I thanked the hostess, who had bought three books—probably out of pity. Then I loaded 39 damp books in my truck and drove home in the pounding rain. I laughed most of the way, and only cried a little bit.

Now, take one or two of the stories you've already written and go over them with these detail-ideas in mind. Could you have used a more descriptive word? Should you have given more details? Do your word-choices truly reflect how you felt about the event you described? NOTE: Be willing to delete those blah-blah-blah sections that come into almost every story. Here it helps to have a good friend who will read your story and tell you the truth.

It's time to write another story with these points in mind. Choose one of these topics (or another one altogether):

A time when I wasn't at my best

A day I wish I'd stayed in bed

A moment when someone unexpectedly showed me a new way of accomplishing something

Have fun with it!

Chapter 11 – The Letter I Wish I'd Written

In one of the earlier chapters I mentioned the woman whose teenaged and young adult children "would never read anything that wasn't on their phones." Well, if that's the sort of problem you have too, keep in mind that there are multiple ways of recording any story. In a text, an email, an attachment to either of those, a computer file, a vocal recording—or the old-fashioned but still viable way of using pencil and paper. The choice is completely yours. Pick whatever works for you.

The same goes for our topic today – a letter. The format you use to compose it doesn't matter, although there *are* some points you might want to consider.

Yes. Texts and emails are quicker. But just think of what someone in the future may feel when they hold in their hands the letter you've written. Just by itself, the paper will show whether the letter was read and re-read, folded and re-folded, kept in a pocket or purse and scuffed by the other contents therein. Or will the paper still be pristine? Will that indicate that the recipient ignored the letter, resented it, never read it, *or* treasured it so much they kept it as clean and tidy as they possibly could?

The answer? Nobody knows. But the clues will be provocative, wouldn't you say?

So, why are we talking about writing a letter today? Not just any old letter. This will be a letter to express things that you've left unspoken. You may have some ideas that spring instantly to mind—or you may need to mull this over a bit.

There are many reasons for not having said something:
 I was too busy
 It didn't seem quite the right time
 I didn't know how to introduce the topic
 I didn't feel safe telling that person how I felt
 I was embarrassed about bringing it up
 I simply didn't think about saying it back then
 My feelings were so intense I was afraid to let them spill out
 I didn't realize how important it was until it was too late

And why write a letter anyway?
 To thank someone

To apologize
To clear the air of a misunderstanding
To express anger or wonder or regret
To question someone
To explain your actions
To express or ask for forgiveness
To say goodbye

Remember that this is the letter you *wish* you'd written. The one that you never got around to. Well, I'm here to tell you that there will never be a better time than now. You can do it. Write a date. Write the salutation (Dear …)

You don't want to call the person *dear*? That's okay. You don't have to. Try putting their name inside the first sentence, like this:

I decided to write you today, NAME, to let you know that … and so on.

After you've written your letter, you have several options:
        Send it (mail, email, text, post)
        Keep it (there are several reasons for this option, which I'll discuss in a moment)
        Give it to someone else to read (choose this person very carefully)
        Burn it and assume the message will get through somehow or other

Keep in mind it's the *writing* that's important. You don't necessarily have to send the letter. In fact, there are instances where it would be better if you didn't even consider sending it. Remember that AA step about making amends. If your letter will open old wounds—will harm the recipient—it's better just to ignore the post office or the internet. I ignored my own advice a couple of years ago and sent a letter trying to explain why I had felt as I had for so many years, and my extended family is still feeling the angry repercussions. It was my fault, and I can't see a way to apologize enough for my impetuous action.

Write to your childhood nemesis to express how you have finally learned to stand up for yourself. Write the spouse who left you and thank them for freeing you to find your second spouse—the love of your life.

As an example, I once wrote a letter to my mother. At this point she had advanced dementia and couldn't possibly have grasped what the letter meant, but I was fairly sure she would grasp the anger it expressed. I was still struggling through counseling to resolve a lot of those issues I had (remember the sense of perspective in Chapter 3?) and felt I needed to give voice to the anger I'd carried for years. I chose to show the letter to my father, and we ended up having a long discussion. "How could you have stood her all these years?" I asked him. And he replied, "I married her for better or for worse, and I stand by my promises." That discussion helped him understand me better and definitely helped me understand him more.

There may be other times when you *can't* send the letter, because the addressee is dead. That's okay. Go ahead and write it. Write your old 10th-grade social studies teacher to tell him how many times you've used what you learned in his class, even though he retired 20 years ago and is long-buried. Write to the child you miscarried at five months to tell her how much you still love her. Write your brother who was killed in the war while you were protesting that war at home.

Now, take a few moments to think about those unsaid thoughts. Sometimes it's easiest to begin with a letter of gratitude. Then you can go on to the more difficult ones later.

Who do you wish you'd thanked years ago? Start now.

Dear …

And here's a letter I wrote almost two decades ago:

9-22-2007

My dear Dad,

Remember that summer in the late 1950s when we camped out beside a burbling creek on the side of a Colorado mountain? You started picking up pebbles from the stream bank and tossing them into the middle of the creek. Diana and I joined in the fun, and over the next seven days, we three built a dam, one that the water poured over with surprising force. We took a noisy but slow creek and turned it into a toll booth. The next Saturday we filled in the trench we'd dug for a latrine, picked up all our gear, scattered the remains of our campfires, and left.

We changed the course of the world in that week. How many fish couldn't migrate up or down that stream because of us? How many animals found a blessed pool to bathe or to fish in? Did the water carve out a new path, one around our artificial obstacle? Did soil cave in as a result? Or was new land formed downstream when there wasn't the same flow of water to erode it?

We changed the course of the world that week, as I watched Diana wash her teenaged face in the cold water each morning, as I struggled with handling a fly-fishing pole, as you walked the land beyond the stream and saw such sights and could not tell us what you learned from them.

And when you died, you changed the course of the world that week, as Diana and I sat beside you, and you still could not tell us what you had learned. I wish I had asked my questions sooner, before you forgot how to share. I wish I had asked sooner, before you unlearned your early lessons and learned your new ones. I wish I had listened more, even when you did not speak, for there was the chance that, like a fish nosing through the new pool that appeared overnight, you might have left behind a circle of cleared space for your ideas to hatch in my mind.

When you died, you took with you so much knowledge, so many secrets, but you changed the course of the world that final week of your life, for the thing you did teach me was that death was light and bright and welcoming. And for that, dear Dad, I thank you.

Your loving daughter,
--Fran

It really doesn't matter which of the reasons you choose for why to write your letter. The important thing is to write it. Begin now. Today—now—is the perfect time.

Chapter 12 – Topics to Write About

So far, you've accumulated a whole group of topics for your stories. At least I hope you have. And I hope you've started writing them. But for now, let's look at some specific items that people who follow after you will enjoy knowing.

Choose a place you've lived and describe it in detail.
Here are some questions to answer to get you started writing:

> Dorm, house, trailer, apartment, condo…
> Whole place or just one area…
> Who owned it – you, parent(s), other relative(s), spouse, partner, friend…
> Did it have a: yard (grass, gravel, jungle…) swing (on the porch, from a tree, inside...), garden (flowers or veggies or both, your job or someone else's…), porch, fence, front stoop, back stoop, deck…

You get the idea, right?

Example:
When my children were small, we lived in a two-story house that had the bedrooms downstairs and the living area upstairs. The vaulted twelve-foot ceiling in the living room ended in a wall-full of glass that let in the searing afternoon sun. The high center beam ran along the center of the room. It looked like it was the only thing holding up the sloped roof.

It was way too tempting a beam. All we needed was a TALL stepladder and a lot of nerve. Plus two sturdy eye-rings. A drill. A sanded plank for a seat. And plenty of rope.

Of course, we had to move the couch and the end tables out of the way.

The rope went through the eye-rings and fastened with a bowline knot that wouldn't tighten and (more importantly) wouldn't come undone.

Drill holes in the plank, thread the rope through them, fasten well. Test it out. Add children one at a time.

Great fun!

Fran Stewart

It doesn't necessarily have to be a place where *you* lived. This next story is about my dad. I wanted to describe the corn crib on the farm where he grew up. See if you can envision the place:

When my dad was about 10 years old, he and his brothers were playing, the way they often did, in the barn. At the far end of the wagon pass-through lane that ran the length of the inside of the barn was a corncrib that was, unfortunately and unremittingly, infested with rats.

Imagine this layout: the corncrib was built up off the ground level. To get into it, there was a door that opened outward. Just inside that door there was a partially enclosed step about 8" wide and maybe 6" from top to bottom.

The goal of the game was for the boys to listen through the door until they heard a rat on that inner step, gnawing on the corn kernels that inevitably fell into that area. Then they'd take turns whipping open the door, grabbing the rat right behind the head, and then flinging it really hard to snap its neck.

That was a lot more fun than the rat eradication programs the county instituted that involved multiple poisons.

The only trouble was that one day, my dad grabbed a big ole tough rat too far back. The rat twisted around and bit right into his hand at the base of his thumb. And held on! The only way Dad could dislodge the rat was to fling his hand as hard as he could—which worked, because the rat fell to the ground. But it took a big chunk of flesh with it.

"I ran faster than I'd ever run up to the house, yelling for Mama all the way."

"What did she do?"

"She took a big can of turpentine, poured a bunch of it into a bowl, and stuck my hand in it. She had to kill all the rat germs." He rubbed the scar that stilled showed on his right hand. "It probably saved my life."

"Oh, Dad, the pain must have been awful. What did you do?"

He looked at me like he thought I was nuts. "I cried."

Choose a person you know and describe them in detail.

Relative, stranger, friend, enemy...

Age relative to yourself at the time you knew or encountered them (older, younger, same, unknowable...)

Salient physical characteristics (include specific details, but only if they're relevant to your story)

When they smiled, was it tentative, glowing, fake? Was it loving or was it a sneer?

Why they were/are important to you (what impact they made on your life, what insights you learned from them...)

If you'd like an **example**, here's another from my own memoirs:

She walked her last step in 1947, the year I was born. My parents, who had been freed by the Air Force to a life away from their own parents, adopted her as their "Mother."

Her daughter, whom I called Aunt Lucille, cared for her. Uncle Martin carried her from car to wheelchair, from wheelchair to bed. We lived next-door to them at Shaw Field, South Carolina.

As her eyesight declined over the years, she still saw my ash-brown hair as the blondish curls I'd sported as a four-year-old. She always called me her "golden-haired angel." When my dad received his orders to ship out to Germany in 1952, Uncle Martin was assigned to the same airfield. They went ahead to open the base. We females followed months later and ended up once more as close neighbors in the base housing.

Mother Ebbesen told me once, when I stayed with them during my mother's month-long hospital stay, that she would have gone insane without her needlework. I sat with her hour after hour and watched her push a thick embroidery needle through a tablecloth with a pre-printed cross-stitch design. Once the needle was shoved completely through the fabric, Mother Ebbesen grasped the entire tablecloth between her forearms, turned it upside down, found the needle. She took the needle between claw-like fingers that pointed sideways almost ninety degrees from her wrist bones and a thumb that bent in a permanent capital L and pulled it to tug the thread through to the end of its allotted length. Next, she grasped the cloth again with her forearms to turn it upright. I was always fascinated by how well she guided the needle from the back to pierce up through the white cloth at the beginning of the next cross-stitch. Then she'd pull her right arm to one side and lift it to the top side of the fabric, pick up the needle with meticulous skill, and pull the thread through once more. Then she started the entire routine again for the next tiny cross.

After Mother Ebbesen died, Aunt Lucille gave me two of her hand-stitched aprons, and two dish towels. I treasure those items, but the true gifts that Mother Ebbesen left me have proven to be far more important. She taught me the value of patience. She corrected my manners. She showed me that age need not erase delight.

She taught my father to do cross-stitch, urging him to put one mistake into the pattern so it would be truly his. She tried to teach me more advanced techniques than mere cross-stitch, but I was much more interested in playing hide and seek with her. Bent with rheumatoid arthritis, unable to walk, she was the best—and sneakiest—hide and seek playmate I've ever had. The rule was that we couldn't hide in any place we wouldn't truly fit. Not in the breadbox, nor in the oven. The toilet was out of bounds, as was the three-inch space beneath the couch. The other rule was absolute honesty. If I found her—or if she found me—we had to 'fess up and admit defeat. To this day I play that form of mental hide and seek with my grandchildren, and I find it to be one of the most valuable legacies I ever received.

Okay. Do your writing about either of these topics (or both of them!) and then proceed to these next suggestions:

What sort of kindness have you been shown? When did this happen to you? Who precipitated it? How much did you need it at the time? Did it change your life in any way?

The corollary to this, of course, is "When have you shown kindness to someone else?" Why did you do it? How did it change your life?

What are you looking forward to? Long term, short term, what do you expect to get out of it?

Funny moments that you enjoy remembering. This one speaks for itself—but be sure to include pertinent details. Remember that laughter from the heart can bind people together.

Example (again, from my own memoirs)
Gingerbread Houses

The table in our new house was enormous. Not just long, but wide as well. It had perhaps been a mistake designing it that way, although the way the surface matched the kitchen countertops was striking. When we sat for a meal, though, we adults could hardly reach across the expanse. Our children's short arms were even less effective.

So, mealtimes didn't work. But ahh, the possibilities for the holidays!

What better way to inaugurate our first Christmas in that remodeled house than to host a gingerbread party.

You know me. I don't like to cook, so making gingerbread was out of the question. Graham crackers, though, work pretty well as substitute gingerbread. And royal icing to cement the cracker walls together and to attach the decorations was a breeze to make. All I needed was a heavy-duty mixer, lots of powdered sugar, and a kazillion egg whites. And yes, we ate scrambled eggs from frozen egg yolks for weeks afterward.

We invited practically everyone we knew and asked them all to bring candy for decorating. Then we pooled all those offerings together in the middle of the table, which we had covered with taped-down aluminum foil (shiny side up). M&Ms, mints, licorice strings, peppermint in all sorts of forms, candy canes, gumdrops, chocolate in a million different shapes and sizes, pretzels.

A Mounds Bar made a great canoe in the little lake formed by letting the aluminum foil show in the middle of white icing snowbanks.

The stick pretzels formed fences and gates and arbors. The pretzel-shaped mini-pretzels were great for whimsical windows, for roof decorations, for paving walkways between the houses.

Our village slowly evolved over the whole table. One enterprising person whom I liked despite the fact that she tended to be a bit preachy, created a church that dominated the center. The licorice-string cross on top of its steeple was a masterful stroke of engineering.

Not to be outdone, one of the latecomers to the party took one look at that church and set about creating a "business district" to go beside it. She inveigled other guests into making a grocery store, a shopping mall (a very small one, since I was close to running out of graham crackers by that point), a hardware store. Her crowning touch, though, was the business she created without any help from anyone. Eventually we all stopped doing anything else and simply watched her.

The balcony that ran along the front of the upstairs floor featured a gumdrop woman with several prominent M&Ms on her chest leaning over the pretzel railing, gesturing with her red licorice arms to a gumdrop man on the street below her. There was no sign advertising the place, but there WAS a bright red candy "light" over the front door.

She placed it right next-door to the church.

Fran Stewart

And now, for some more questions
As I mentioned in the acknowledgments to this book, I've been a long-time fan of artist Lyn Asselta's weekly email newsletter. Several months ago, she published a list of questions along with her usual thoughtful reflections about life. I asked for her permission to quote her in my classes, and now I've received permission to include two of her essays in this book. Every single one of these questions she asks can be a memoirs topic. I'd suggest that you answer them one at time in any order whatsoever.

from Lyn Asselta's "Saturdays at the Cove"
newsletter 11/9/24
(used with her permission)

What is my purpose?
What do I contribute?
Who can I love?
What are my limitations?
What are my strengths?
Am I kind?
Can I be brave?
What can I accept?
If I grieve, what is the source of my grief?
What have I learned?
What am I learning now?
Who can I help?
How can I help?
What can I share?
What am I grateful for?
What do I fear?
What do I hide?
What leaves me speechless?
How can I be better?
What will I leave behind?

Life is a test, isn't it? It is an ongoing series of questions that we each must answer in our own words, a series of complexities we must confront individually, time and time again, if we are to contribute in a positive way to this world. The answers for each of us are different, derived from our life experiences, our cultures, our personal interests, individual needs, and any number of other factors.

If we're so inclined, we can make up our own questions in this test called Life. Different questions may be relevant at different times and under different circumstances. We can add questions or subtract them at will, depending on how introspective we feel. But we are each on the honor system to complete the answers and to refrain from copying, cheating, or skipping the test altogether.

There is no time limit for this test called Life.

New questions may appear unexpectedly at any time.

No two tests will have the same questions.

One-word answers will be sufficient for some, but complete sentences and paragraphs will carry more weight.

If necessary, you may erase and change your answers at any time.

You will be responsible for grading your own test. Begin.

***

To sign up for Lyn's Saturday newsletter, simply go to her website (lynasselta. com), click on the *Email Newsletter* tab and add your name and email address.

Have I given you enough fodder to keep you busy for quite a while?

Fran Stewart

Chapter 13 – Meaning, Goals, Purpose

Lyn's questions at the end of the last chapter lead us right into the topics for this one.

In my classes I used to give people a little chart where they could list "Three Things I'd Like to Do / Be / or Have," but I found out gradually (I can be a very slow learner at times) that these questions simply aren't relevant to people who have reached a certain age. We have different priorities, even though we still have things we'd like to do before we croak. We're more likely to be trying to get rid of the "stuff" we've accumulated over the past decades rather than looking to accumulate more.

So, I came up with this new list of Three Things:

1. What is the meaning of my life today?
2. What goals do I still want to meet?
3. What is my purpose in life?

You can take them one at a time and spend as long as you need to in mulling over the answers—or, even better, you can jump right in and register your first thoughts about each of these. Remember, you can always go back and change your wording, add new ideas, delete those impulsive comments you don't want to regret later.

Next, I'd like you to think more deeply about your goals. Answer the following two questions about each one of them:

1. How do I see myself (or how do others see me) now before I've accomplished this goal?
2. How will I feel when I've achieved or accomplished this?

It's time to write!

Fran Stewart

Chapter 14 – Have I Ever Been …

Now let's look at specific moments in our life that we can be proud of.
When I was brave …
When I lived up to a challenge ...
And then there's the other side of the coin, since every life has positive and negative aspects.

Explore your perceptions of your more negative side by asking
Have I ever been insincere?
Have I ever been monstrous, thoughtless?
Have I ever been arrogant?
Have I ever been cowardly?

Can you think of other questions that would fit here? Remember once again that the stories you tell now may help people years from now to feel as if they are not alone. That's a lovely gift to leave, wouldn't you say?

One of the best bits of advice given in self-help workshops is this:
Act as if, and you will become.
If we're not in the place we'd like to be—if we're not brave, if we're not compassionate, if we're not adventuresome—then *acting as if we are* can help us to overcome those obstacles. This does NOT mean to go out and try to wrestle a crocodile, but it may mean taking a walk in cold weather, volunteering at a homeless shelter, or accepting that invitation to go tent camping.

Then—naturally—write about it!

Do Not Fall
by Lyn Asselta © 2024

Do not fall for the commonplace.
Do not.
Fall instead for those things that lift it up,
the things that pull it from its weary station.
Fall for the way sunlight dances on the wavy windows of old barns
and the way tall grass weaves between their weathered clapboards.
Fall for the smell of wild roses, far from perfection,

but whose fragrance has not been stripped away in favor of their
size.
Fall for the faded chair, worn and sagging from long reads
and cups of tea
and deep conversations late at night.
Fall for the homemade, the handiwork,
the pride that comes of creating.
Fall for the unique.
Fall for the history, the humanity,
the courage of things.
Do not fall for the must-haves, the popular, the trendy, the ordinary.
Fall instead for integrity, for purpose,
for the undeniably beautiful truth of things.

***

To sign up for Lyn's Saturday newsletter, simply go to her website (lynasselta. com), click on the *Email Newsletter* tab and add your name and email address.

* * *

Chapter 15 - Dilemmas

Have you ever come up against a real dilemma in your life? Have you ever even thought about such a thing? Choosing between right and wrong or between good and evil is no choice at all. We will always choose what we perceive as good or what we think is right. Notice the careful wording of that sentence. Those around us may interpret our actions as wrong or as evil, but we are always the hero in our own play. Our idea of "good" may involve the greater good for our family or our nation—or it may simply be the "good" of protecting our own interests, be they selfish or otherwise. But still, there is no dilemma involved in such a choice.

A **dilemma** would be choosing between two irreconcilable goods or the lesser of two inevitable evils. Did you see the movie *Sophie's Choice*? If so, you know that's a good example of a dilemma, in which Sophie was compelled in a Nazi concentration camp to choose which of her two children is to be killed immediately and which is to live. And then she had to live with that decision.

I doubt that many of us have been up against such a heart-rending choice, but we may very well have experienced decisions as a care-taker: do we refuse to pull the plug and possibly condemn a loved one to months of agony or drug-induced stupor while we wait for an uncertain cure? Or do we allow for life termination only to feel that we could have / should have waited?

It could be something simpler, such as deciding which college to attend, which profession to enter, which person to continue a relationship with.

It's time now to explore any <u>dilemmas</u> in your life.

Write about what led you to have to make such a choice.

Were there any other conceivable options?

What were the pros and cons of each choice?

What did you ultimately decide, and why?

Were you okay with that decision, or have you spent (wasted) time second guessing yourself?

By the same token, if you're facing a dilemma *now*, writing about it may help to clarify your mind.

Fran Stewart

Chapter 16 – Getting in Trouble

When did you get in the most trouble? What happened to precipitate the event? Just how much trouble? Would you do it again if you could? I remember the old Dennis the Menace cartoon where he sits in the corner, looks at his teddy bear, and says, "It was worth it!"

The people reading your stories years from now will want the juicy details. Be willing to let yourself be vulnerable. We've all gotten in trouble, whether it's something big or something minor. Go ahead— tell about the BIG trouble. Was it an honest, unintended mistake on your part, or did you plan it out ahead of time? Was it downright illegal or just an error in judgement? Did you come out of it relatively unscathed—or did someone end up getting hurt (and you've been plagued by that memory for all these years)? Is it just a memory, or were there substantial consequences?

This chapter can also encompass stories about our ancestors. When they got in trouble. What they were up against in their lives. How they dealt with daily problems.

These may not be *your* stories directly, but they *are* stories that have affected your life in one way or another. The stories you hear about people you never met, or people you knew only when they were old, old, old – these are stories that give you a sense of your place in the universe. They help to define who you are, because they reflect where you came from.

Do you know any ancestor stories about getting in trouble?

These stories can be as mild as the one I shared about my dad being careless enough to be bitten by the rat, or as socially unacceptable as that other story I shared about his having been responsible for a man's death.

Write, write, write.

Fran Stewart

Chapter 17 -- Wrapping it up: Final Thoughts

I'd like to end all this with some open-ended questions that you might want to answer and consider including in your stories. You can stick them in anywhere they seem to fit. Maybe include a new category called "Musings" (see chapter 8 – Organizing Your Stories).

1. Human beings are here to…

2. I am on this earth to…

3. Wholeness means…

4. God is…

5. Prayer is…

6. Justice requires…

7. Evil happens when…

8. My three core values are...

9. My two most influential "spiritual mentors"

10. The belief I am questioning (or have questioned) the most

That's it for now. There's no further assignment except to keep up with writing and preserving your all-important stories.

What you write today may be a roadmap for future generations.

I wish you the very best, and hope to hear from you,

--Fran

Fran Stewart

Chapter 18 – Other Stories

And now, I'm going to share with you some of my favorite memoirs stories. The last one is a collection of three posts I put on my franstewartauthor Facebook page back in February of 2015 after I came close to dying. I hope you'll find it well worth reading. Don't bother looking for me on Facebook, by the way; I cancelled my account as a protest to the way social media has been politically skewed.

My Earliest Memory – Types of Flight

Although my sister argues with me about the length of the staircase and the fact of the piano bench, who is she to mess with my memory?

We lived in a second-floor apartment somewhere, Tennessee I think, but at four the names of states meant nothing to me. The staircase, though, I remember well. It was long. It was steep. Very long and very steep. Why our parents left us up there, I'll never know. They'd gone to visit with the people in the first-floor apartment. I remember wrapping my fingers around a white spindle to my left and canting my right arm out to balance me as I reached far down that first step. Then I had to let go with my left hand and find one more point of purchase, the next security spindle.

When my heel slipped on the edge of the second tread, that first wondering moment felt somehow like flight. I looked to my left and saw the white spindles flowing upward and behind me in a dizzying parade as I slid feet-first down the staircase runway—light, shadow, light, shadow, white, space, white, space, wood, air, wood, air, bright, dark, bright, dark, thump, bump, thump.

My bottom and my spine took the brunt of my inadvertent flight, a downward journey controlled only by gravity and whatever angels hover around small children as they learn about spatial orientation and test the length of their small limbs.

I remember—I truly do—the pale-yellow light that oozed around the grownups from the door behind them as their faces seemed to waver above me. They laid me on a piano bench. A piano bench it was. Or maybe a coffee table; but it was the size of a piano bench. The light was brighter there with the lampshade taken off. "I don't think anything's broken," somebody said.

I don't remember any bruises, although I can't imagine how I could have seen my own back anyway. In fact, other than the piano bench, the light, the voice, I don't recall any of the aftermath. To this day, though, I love to recreate that flight, to drive south down a highway lined with tall pine trees in the bright mid-morning, passing through alternating lines of sun and shadow, bright and dark, wood, air, wood, air, flashing by on my left, but with no thump, bump, thump at the end of this controlled flight.

* * *

Who/What/Where I Left Behind

My tiger toy,
A broken doll,
A shriveled tube of toothpaste in the dorm.

My grandparents,
Piano lessons,
The dog my mother killed when I was twelve.

My big pink bear,
And yearbooks (four),
The boy I left but might have truly loved.

Black Stallion
Little Women,
A weedy garden and a butcher knife.

A bright green car,
The winter snow,
Five houses where I'd somehow left my mark.

Half a ton
of rocks, a comb,
My uterus, and a roommate in a twit.

Six dead loved cats,
A TV set,
The mountains in Colorado and Vermont.

A job or two,
A sparkly dress,
The hair that hung below my shoulder blades.

* * *

Fran Stewart

Why I'm a Dandelion

I am a dandelion. As a child of an Air Force family, I learned early on that I could bloom just about anywhere I was planted.

My colors are brightest in the spring and early summer, but with the autumn I grow white-headed, and in winter I hunker down waiting for spring again.

I gleefully spread my joy along the winds of chance, I nourish the bees, I give delight to those who want to blow their thoughts through my head, but I am never quelled by winds that try to shake me.

* * *

My Too-Late Note

Monday - 04/26/2021 — A couple of weeks ago, I tried to make contact with someone only to find that the phone number I had didn't work and the email I sent her bounced back. So I Googled her. And found her obituary.

The good intention a number of months too late. How often does that happen? If only I'd contacted her sooner. If only … if only …

Here's the email I tried to send, and below it is her poem that so impressed me.

> Nell, I was just looking through my old copy of the 2018 Atlanta anthology and re-read your poem "From the Deck."
>
> I tried to call you to let you know how lovely it was to rediscover such a jewel of writing, but the phone number I had wouldn't go through.
>
> Your words—"morning's holy prize"—reminded me so much of what I feel each morning when I take my tea out to my front porch and watch the dawn. Occasionally I find deer (with their "exclamation ears") in my yard, and when I do, I feel a kinship with you through your exquisitely phrased words.
>
> So, I just want to thank you.

From the Deck
©Nell Abbott

Down through the layered limbs of green
where morning spills its bits of sun,
she comes.

Fran Stewart

Brown as the leaves she tiptoes through
with dancer's lift of leg and hoof,
she comes.

Brushing aside the redbud leaves,
the lovely valentine redbud leaves,
she finds the seeds.

The greedy birds have left her few
and as I lift my cooling cup,
her head comes up.

Her exclamation ears point up.
Her eyes find mine, hers wild and wise
and unafraid,

The way all creatures must have stared
through Eden's mists before harm came.
And so ...

She gives me morning's holy prize,
that with each dawn's redemptive skies
our souls are born.

* * *

The Pool: Aftermath to Divorce

Five years old and three feet tall. Well, three and a half feet. The shallow end of the swimming pool was four feet deep. Tippy-toes and a tilted back head kept my nose and most of my chin above water, most of the time. My sister at the deep end with her friends jumping in, splashing.

The ripples charging from there to where I was, threatening my precarious connection to air. Me? Hugging the rough concrete wall, scraping the skin off my toes, trying to hang on.

Forty-five years old and five-foot-seven. In over my head for the past twenty-four years. Floundering, hanging on with my chin in the air and heart on hold in the swamp.

A year later, letting go of the wall, dog-paddling out, alone, splashing water up my nose, gulping mouthfuls, spitting it out, floundering, learning to float from sheer necessity. Reaching out with one tentative arm, then another, combing the sea of doubt, plowing the ocean of my discomfort, sounding the waves, pummeled by the surf. Finding a dolphin, a sea turtle, a gray whale who mothers me, who binds up my scraped toes and washes my eyes with clear water, who helps me unlearn the floundering and shows me that swimming is much more fun.

* * *

83

Joy

Last night I took my eight-year-old granddaughter to see *A Midsummer Night's Dream* at the Shakespeare Tavern in Atlanta. It was an entirely selfish move on my part. I have two grown children who don't care much for Shakespeare. I have a number of friends who don't want to be bothered. I have one friend who loves Shakespeare, but whose physical limitations frequently prevent her—at the last minute—from attending, even though we have reserved tickets.

Savannah Joy, though, she's a completely different factor in the equation. Three years ago I asked her, "Do you think you'd like to go with Grannie to see the Shakespeare plays when you get to be ten years old?"

"Yes," she assured me with five-year-old certainty. "Yes I would."

Despite how often I've tried to curb my impatience, I couldn't wait any longer. Three weeks ago, on a regular Tuesday-with-Grannie, I asked her if she thought she was ready to see a Shakespeare play. A jack-in-the-box response from her assured me that my request had an affirmative.

"Okay," I said. "Next Tuesday, bring seventeen of your small stuffed animals to Grannie's house."

She raised an eyebrow—even at eight, she's good at that—but complied none-the-less. Seventeen stuffed toys in a Walmart bag, hanging from a coat hook until ten a.m. or so. "Are we ready for Shakespeare?" I asked.

"Maybe after some cheese," her ever-hungry younger brother insisted. "Hard cheese."

I shaved thin slices of Parmigiano Reggiano for him and some chewy Mozzarella for Savannah, with a few slices of each for Grannie.

Clean up the counter, wash the cutting board, knife, and plate, wipe hands again, and haul out a clean sheet to spread on the floor. While Savannah dumped the stuffed animals out and spread them-about, I gathered up the strips of paper on which I'd printed the names of old Bill's characters in a 36-point font. Taking up the first slip, I said, "Theseus is a duke in the city of Athens. He's a general, and he's kind of a tough guy."

Savannah dithered a bit and selected a brown bear. With my handy stock of straight pins, I stuck *Theseus* onto the top of the bear's head.

"Hippolyta," I explained, "is the Queen of the Amazons. She is a warrior queen, very strong, very powerful, very sure of herself. She and Theseus were warring against each other, but when they met, they fell in love, and now they've stopped their war, and they're planning on getting married in the next four days."

A graceful giraffe took Hippolyta's label in stride.

"Now, in comes Egeus, dragging his daughter Hermia. He wants Hermia to marry Demetrius, but she loves Lysander."

Egeus was assigned to a wrinkled white Georgia bulldawg. Hermia—I had to inform Savannah that Hermia was quite short. That's important later in the play. The *Hermia* label goes on a miniature dachshund.

Demetrius becomes a tall turtle, and *Lysander* is applied to a fuzzy brown doggie.

As I explain that Egeus insists that the Duke force Hermia to marry Demetrius, Savannah becomes incensed—rightly so, to my mind. And when Egeus demands the death penalty for her refusal to obey him, Savannah mentally joins forces with Hippolyta's indignation at such a stupid Athenian law.

Then Helena, a rangy gray puppy in a tutu, runs off to tell Demetrius that Hermia and Lysander are planning to run away to get married. She follows him to the woods, as he follows Hermia.

As I went through the story, moving the various animals on and off the stage—and, of course, in *A Midsummer Night's Dream*, there's a lot of moving on and offstage—Savannah followed the story beautifully.

She laughed at the thought of the rustic workmen—three teddy bears, a dog, and two bunnies—practicing the play *Pyramus and Thisbe* for the Duke's wedding day.

She decided the fairy Peaseblossom was about the funniest critter ever thought of, and matched my own disdain for Oberon, the fairy king who wanted to steal Titania's young ward. She watched in delight as Puck raced around the world three times to gather the flower that would enchant Titania's eyes, to make her fall in love with a monster when she awoke. And she gasped in horror when Puck placed the flower juice in Lysander's eyes by mistake, causing him to awake and see Helena. Now the fuzzy brown doggie and the tall green turtle are both pursuing the floppy gray pup-in-a-tutu around the wood, leaving the poor dachshund Hermia alone and afraid.

We had quite a discussion about the use of the word *ass,* since it is, after all, an integral part of the play. Savannah decided that she could listen to it, but it probably would be best if she didn't quote it to anyone except Grannie and maybe her Mommy.

After we'd seen Titania, quite an elegant rabbit, make a fool of herself over Bottom the weaver, and Oberon stole the boy and reversed the spell on Titania's eyes, we came to the finale, as all three couples married, and then sat to watch the play within a play. Savannah chuckled mightily as Grannie described Bottom pulling out a wooden sword and dying at great length, and laughed over the wordplay of rhyming *good* with *blood.* Naturally, I was in my element.

After only a little coaxing, Savannah agreed to tell the story back to me. She peeked at the tags occasionally but had an amazing grasp of the flow of the story. With very little prompting, she traced the shenanigans of the Athenians, the fairies, and the royals. Yes! We finally folded all the critters up in the sheet, stowed it away in Grannie's office where the cats couldn't get at it, and rewarded ourselves with a play bout in the sand boxes on the back deck.

The next Tuesday, Savannah suggested that we take off all the tags and reassign the characters "to different actors." Again, we went through the story, this time with me reading bits and pieces of the dialogue, so she could get used to the language.

Finally, Friday night, last night arrived. I picked her up early and drove to the city at a leisurely pace. We shared Rainy Day Tomato Soup with Zucchini Bread, and Cornish Pasty, the original Elizabethan meat pie that theater-goers in the 1500s ate. One quick trip to the bathroom, and we were ready for the play to begin. The next few hours were heaven. Savannah laughed and giggled and gasped and wheezed. She bounced up and down with delight. She guffawed at times and frowned mightily at others.

Intermission featured a bowl of yummy ice cream and a visit by the head of the Shakespeare Company Volunteers who asked Savannah if she was enjoying the play. Upon Savannah's enthusiastic response, Mrs. Mercer said, "If you can wait a bit after the play, I'd be happy to give you a tour of the backstage."

Well, heaven just kept going. Although I've loved the Shakespeare Tavern for years, I saw it joyously through new eyes last night, the eyes of an eight-year-old just discovering a world of magic and delight.

We're already making plans for next month.

* * *

Somebody Said a Mother ...

I found this somewhere on the internet years ago. Although I can't give credit to the person who wrote it, I felt it was important enough to leave for my grandchildren to read someday as they have children of their own.

Somebody Said ...

Somebody said a mother is an unskilled laborer
. . . somebody never gave a squirmy infant a bath.

Somebody said it takes about six weeks to get back to normal after you've had a baby
. . . somebody doesn't know that once you're a mother, normal is history.

Somebody said a mother's job consists of wiping noses and changing diapers
. . somebody doesn't know that a child is much more than the shell they live in.

Somebody said you learn how to be a mother by instinct
. . . somebody never took a three-year-old shopping.

Somebody said being a mother is boring
. . . somebody never rode in a car driven by a teenager with a driver's permit.

Somebody said teachers, psychologists, and pediatricians know more about children than their mothers
. . . somebody hasn't invested her heart in another human being.

Somebody said if you're a "good" mother, your child will "turn out"
. . . somebody thinks a child is like a bag of plaster of Paris that comes with directions, a mold, and a guarantee.

Somebody said being a mother is what you do in your spare time
. . . somebody doesn't know that when you're a mother, you're a mother ALL the time.

Somebody said "good" mothers never raise their voices
. . . somebody never came out the back door just in time to see her child wind up and hit a golf ball through the neighbor's kitchen window.

Somebody said you don't need an education to be a mother
. . . somebody never helped a fourth grader with their math.

Somebody said you can't love the fifth child as much as you love the first
. . . somebody doesn't have five children.

Somebody said a mother can find all the answers to her child-rearing questions in the books
. . . somebody never had a child stuff beans up their nose.

Somebody said the hardest part of being a mother is labor and delivery
. . . somebody never watched her "baby" get on the bus for the first day of kindergarten.

Somebody said a mother can do her job with her eyes closed and one hand tied behind her back
. . . somebody never organized seven giggling Brownies to sell cookies.

Somebody said a mother can stop worrying after her child gets married
. . . somebody doesn't know that marriage adds a new son- or daughter-in-law to a mother's heartstrings.

Somebody said a mother's job is done when her last child leaves home.
. . . somebody never had grandchildren.

Fran Stewart

Somebody said being a mother is a side dish on the plate of life
. . . somebody doesn't know what fills you up.

Somebody said your mother knows you love her, so you don't need
to tell her
. . . somebody isn't a mother.

* * *

Yellow Angel Stories

United Flight Attendant Saved My Life

2/1/2015 – This banyan tree at Wailuku River State Park has formed a grove – all attached, all one tree, but when I threw up my hands in sheer glory, I was standing between the root-joined trees in a clearing that was well more than a hundred feet in diameter. It was the holiest ground I've ever stood on. I'm glad I contacted that energy on that particular day.

A few hours later, I was on an airplane headed to Houston. I couldn't sleep well throughout that night flight, and about two hours outside of Houston I began to be very uncomfortable. When the flight attendants came around with morning juices, I told one of them that I was having trouble breathing. He brought me a tank of oxygen. With the mask on my face, I began to feel much better. Another attendant came by and asked if I'd like to be checked by paramedics when we landed. "No, I'm breathing just fine now." You see, I knew a paramedic visit would mean nobody else could get off the plane until the "problem" had been handled. I didn't want anyone to miss a flight because of me – and I had only an hour layover before my flight home.

She came back a few minutes later. "The pilot says we'll be

arriving 15 minutes early. Are you sure you don't want to see a para-medic?"

"No, really." I took two deep breaths. "I'm doing okay now."

A few minutes later she was back again. "May I take your pulse?" I lifted my arm. Within seconds she had both her hands on mine. "If you've had trouble on this big plane," she said, "you won't enjoy the next flight. It's on what we in the industry call a Barbie Doll plane – it's real skinny and bounces all over the place." Before I could object (again), she said, "Honey, I'd feel a whole lot better if you let me call the paramedics. Would you do it just for me? Please?"

So I said yes.

Turns out my pulse was bouncing between 174 and 90, back up to 128, 70, 163, 35. And the EKG looked like an earthquake had hit.

That flight attendant had figured out exactly how to get me to do what she felt was necessary. She saved my life. I don't know her name, but she was on United Flight 252 Honolulu to Houston on January 26/27 (overnight). If you know any of the crew on that flight, please pass the word on. Better yet, please share this post with anyone you know – the word is bound to get to her eventually.

I have to go take a nap now. I'll be back sometime to tell you the rest of the story.

~ ~ ~

Yellow Angel

2/3/2015 – As soon as the paramedics saw my heart going crazy on the EKG, one of them said, "We're taking you to the hospital, ma'am."

"No! I have a flight to Atlanta in less than an hour."

He looked at me long and hard, all the while packing up his little EKG machine. "No, ma'am. You have an ambulance to catch in less than two minutes."

The ER at Memorial Hermann Northeast Hospital was a scramble of activity, but I lay in a fog as they X-rayed my heart, did a CT scan, took blood and urine, and who knows what else. At that point, I didn't care. I felt so exhausted and hurt so much, I didn't see how I could keep going.

Eventually, there came a lull, in which I was left alone in a blessedly quiet room. With no warning sounds whatsoever, I felt a being, a presence, a *something* standing at my left knee. I opened my eyes and saw a column of the most unearthly yellow, swirling gently all the way up to the ceiling and beyond. I felt a sense of ineffable peace. There was no face, there were no arms, no human form whatsoever, but it said to me—did I actually hear it with my ears? I don't think so—but it somehow said, "Don't be afraid. You are at a crossroads in your life, as you have been four previous times. You are completely at choice. You may go with me, or you may stay."

Oh.

I lay there, watching the gently undulating yellow column, and thought about it. I thought perhaps that if I went, I might not hurt so much. I wondered what sort of legacy, if any, I would leave behind. I have two wonderful, loving, happy children, five loving grandchildren, and many dear friends. My 11 published books—soon to be 12—would live on after me. Not a bad record.

I felt content.

Then, just by my left shoulder, I saw a column of the brightest, most vivid purple—as otherworldly a color as the yellow was. It began to roll lists of names upward, like the credits on a movie screen.

My children and grandchildren came first, my closest friends, people whose company I enjoy thoroughly, people I knew many years ago, like Diane Marie Hart, my best friend in 4th grade (whom I've never seen or heard from since then). The list went on and on.

Off to one side of the "credits," the names of my books began to appear, and I saw below them a blank space. Which meant to me that I had a lot more books to write.

I looked back at the yellow angel, who simply waited. There was no feeling of hurry whatsoever. I have no idea whether this process took 2 seconds or 2 hours—it felt timeless.

"I think I'll stay."

A surge of absolute acceptance flooded around and through me. I knew in that moment, that no matter which choice I'd made, the yellow angel would have seen it as exactly right. I have never felt so completely loved in all my life.

The colors dissolved away, and a doctor knocked on the door and entered the room. "We've found the source of your problem," she said. "Your thyroid has gone haywire, which is what's made your heart race for so long, but we can control them both with medication."

I know, I thought.

She obviously thought I was missing the point, so she held her thumb and index finger almost touching. "When you got here, you were that far away from a fatal heart attack."

I know, I thought again, and noticed a tiny yellow prick of light over her shoulder. A reflection? Or a reminder?

* * *

I should note that: a) nothing like this has ever happened to me before; b) I'm fairly sure the angel that appeared to me as a column of bright yellow might appear to someone else with wings or a sword, a face or a halo; and c) If I'd seen somebody with wings, I'm sure I would have thought I was hallucinating.

~ ~ ~

Emergency Room Pizza

2/4/2015 – After the flight attendant saved my life (see banyan tree post on February 1st) and the angel came (see yellow angel post yesterday), I'd been in the ER for more than half a day. Memorial Hermann Northeast Hospital in Houston was full – they didn't have a bed for me (other than the one I was lying on). My daughter called me repeatedly throughout the day. When she called late that evening, I happened to mention that I must be better because I was hungry.

"They haven't fed you?"

"It's an ER, Veronica. I don't think they do meal service here."

"You tell your nurse right now that you need something to eat."

"Okay, okay. I will." At that point I'd already been there in the ER for almost eleven hours, but I truly hadn't thought about food until Veronica's call.

Just a moment after we ended the call, my nurse walked in. "We're transferring you to the ICU in about an hour—or maybe two—or possibly three. As soon as a bed there is available. I'm sorry you've had to stay down here in the ER for so long."

"Thanks, Joe," I said, "but I'm kinda hungry. Is there any food around?"

He brought me some apple juice and a turkey sandwich, opened the juice, unwrapped the sandwich for me (my hands were still too shaky to manage those tasks), and turned to do something else. As I took my second bite, someone with a phone to her ear walked into the room.

"She's right here ... she's eating ... she has a sandwich ... don't worry, we're feeding her ... okay." And she ended the call. "That was your daughter," she said [like I hadn't already figured that out!] "She called to ask for the number of the closest pizza place so she could order you a pizza."

"I'm sorry she took up your time," I said.

"Not at all," she replied. "I think it's sweet. There are so many people here who don't have anyone to worry about them."

So, for the next few days, I told that story to everyone who had a moment to listen. My daughter's loving concern brought smiles to so many faces. I can't tell you how much I appreciate her love and her support. Thank you, Veronica.

* * *

As before, I ask you to share this story with your friends. We all need some light in our lives, whether it comes from caring strangers (like the flight attendant), from caring professionals (like the paramedics and everyone I dealt with at the hospital), from friends (of which I'm thankful to have so many), or from family (who are dearer to me than I could possibly express).

* * *

Now it's time for you to go back and do your own writing ...

Keep in touch,

--Fran

www.ingramcontent.com/pod-product-compliance
Lightning Source LLC
Chambersburg PA
CBHW020948090426
42736CB00010B/1320